Using Windows 8.1

Return of the Start Button

Kevin Wilson

Apress®

Using Windows 8.1: Return of the Start Button

ISBN-13 (pbk): 978-1-4302-6679-2

ISBN-13 (electronic): 978-1-4302-6680-8

Copy Editor: April Rondeau
Compositor: SPi Global
Indexer: SPi Global
Artist: SPi Global
Cover Designer: Anna Ishchenko

Distributed to the book trade worldwide by Springer Science+Business Media New York, 233 Spring Street, 6th Floor, New York, NY 10013. Phone 1-800-SPRINGER, fax (201) 348-4505, email orders-ny@springer-sbm.com, or visit www.springeronline.com. Apress Media, LLC is a California LLC and the sole member (owner) is Springer Science + Business Media Finance Inc (SSBM Finance Inc). SSBM Finance Inc is a **Delaware** corporation.

For information on translations, please email rights@apress.com, or visit www.apress.com.

Apress and friends of ED books may be purchased in bulk for academic, corporate, or promotional use. eBook versions and licenses are also available for most titles. For more information, reference our Special Bulk Sales–eBook Licensing web page at www.apress.com/bulk-sales.

Contents at a Glance

About the Author

Kevin Wilson, a practicing computer engineer and tutor, has had a passion for gadgets, cameras, computers, and technology for many years.

After graduating with a Masters in computer science, software engineering & multimedia systems, he has worked in the computer industry supporting and working with many different types of computer systems, as well as worked in education running specialist lessons on film making and visual effects for young people. He has also worked as an IT tutor, has taught in colleges in South Africa, and has been a tutor for adult education in England.

His books were written in the hope that they will help people to use their computer with greater understanding, productivity, and efficiency—to help students and people in countries like South Africa who have never used a computer before. It is his hope that they will get the same benefits from computer technology as we do.

Acknowledgments

Thanks to all the staff at Apress for their passion, dedication, and hard work in the preparation and production of this book.

To all my friends and family for their continued support and encouragement in all my writing projects.

To all my colleagues, students, and testers who took the time to test procedures and offer feedback on the book.

Finally, thanks to you, the reader, for choosing this book. I hope it helps you to use your computer with greater ease.

Introduction

Using Windows 8.1 introduces you to the new verson of Microsoft Windows and is designed to help beginners and enthusiast users who want to get up and running quickly and make better use of their computers.

Windows 8.1 is a major update from Windows XP, Vista, and Windows 7 and has some radical changes—from the introduction to the Start screen to the desktop and Charms Bar. We explore the fundamentals in this book. Love them or hate them, they're here to stay, so I will do my best to guide you through using your computer with Windows 8.1.

This book has been especially written in a step-by-step fashion using photography and screen prints to illustrate the steps as clearly and concisely as possible.

I hope this book is helpful to you.

CHAPTER 1

■ ■ ■

Setting Up Windows 8

Most PCs will be running some version of Microsoft Windows.

Windows 8 is the latest version of Windows produced by Microsoft and is intended for use on personal computers, such as home and business desktops, laptops, tablets, and media center PCs.

There are significant changes to the operating system, including a new touch-friendly interface with a new Start screen featuring a grid of applications offered with the system. These grid tiles dynamically update.

The Start screen replaces the Start menu of earlier Windows versions, putting more emphasis on touch-screen input.

Windows 8 provides more integration with online services and introduces a new Windows Store, which is where different apps can be downloaded. Free and paid apps are available through the Windows Store. These apps are optimized for touch-screen environments and have a smaller scope in relation to desktop applications.

Windows 8 is available in four versions.

Windows RT is a version of Windows 8 designed specifically for mobile devices such as tablets.

Windows 8 is intended for home users and is most likely installed on your new laptop or PC.

Windows 8 Pro is aimed toward enthusiast users and professional environments such as offices, schools, and colleges.

Windows 8 Enterprise is aimed toward larger business environments and large offices.

Hardware Setup

First, place your machine on a firm desk and insert the battery.

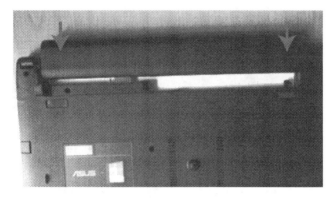

Connect the power cord.

Plug power cord into the side of your laptop or desktop and press the Power button. I will be using my laptop for this example.

USB ports, which you will no doubt come across, let you connect mice, printers, scanners, cameras, and any other accessories you can think of to your computer quickly and easily.

You usually have some USB ports on the back of your machine; these are good for connecting devices you can leave permanently plugged in.

You will also find some USB ports on the front of your machine, which are good for connecting removable media such as external hard disks and USB memory sticks.

Laptops will have USB ports on the sides of the machine.

Upgrading to Windows 8.1

When upgrading from Windows 8, Windows 8 Pro, Windows RT, and any Windows 8.1 Preview versions, the process is the same.

Before you start it is a good idea to make sure all your files, photographs, and music files are backed up onto an external hard disk.

Launch the Windows Store and click "Update to Windows 8.1 for free," which should be on the main page as you launch the Windows Store.

If it isn't on the Store page, you can search for it using the search field on the top right of your screen.

5

windows 8.1 update

| All categories ⌄ | All prices ⌄ | Sort by relevance ⌄ |

On the screen that follows click Download.

The update will begin to download and will install itself in the background, allowing you to keep working in other programs in the meantime. This process is automated and will take some time depending on the speed of your computer and your Internet connection.

Once the download is complete click Restart Now to begin installation. This may take a while.

The computer may reboot a few times while it updates itself.

Starting Windows 8 for the First Time

Once the update is installed and your computer has rebooted, you will be guided through a process similar to the one below, which will allow you to choose some configurations and settings.

Step 1 – Pick a language

As shown in the following screen, you have several choices.

Step 2 – Agree to the license agreement

Once you read the terms, click Accept.

Step 3 – Personalize your copy of Windows 8

Pick a color –I like blue.

PC name – This is useful if you have more than one PC in the house. Good strategy is to name the PC according to either who is using it or what room it's in. I'm going to go with KW-Laptop, because I am using Windows 8 on my laptop. Other examples are ClairesLaptop, PC-Study, PC-livingroom, and so on.

Step 4 – Set up your wireless Internet

Windows 8 will automatically scan for nearby wireless routers. It is just a matter of finding the name of yours in the list. The name of your wireless Internet is called the SSID and will be written on the back of your router.

Step 5 – Configure your settings

I would go with express settings. This allows Windows 8 to configure the settings for you.

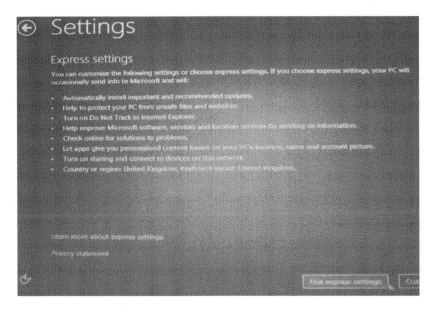

Step 6 – Create a Microsoft account

Click Microsoft Account and follow the instructions on screen. A Microsoft account gives you access to email, the Windows Store, and a lot more than a local account does.

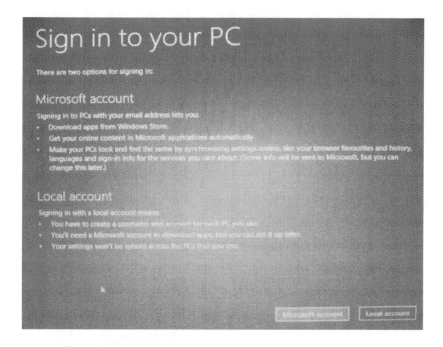

Transferring Files

Now that we're all up and running with Windows 8, you can transfer files from your old machine.

On Your Old Computer

First, connect the external drive to one of the USB ports on your old computer.

If transferring from Windows 7, click on Start and type "Easy Transfer." Under the Programs heading on the search results, click Windows Easy Transfer.

Once Windows Easy Transfer has opened, you will see a screen telling you what Windows Easy Transfer does and what files it transfers. Click Next.

You will need to choose how you want to transfer your files across to your new computer. I recommend using an external hard disk with at least 500GB of space.

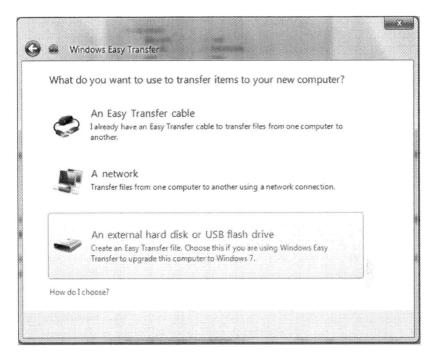

Click on "An external hard disk or USB flash drive."

Next, you need to specify which computer you are using: your old computer or your new computer. Since this machine has all your data on it, it would be your old machine, so click "This is my old computer."

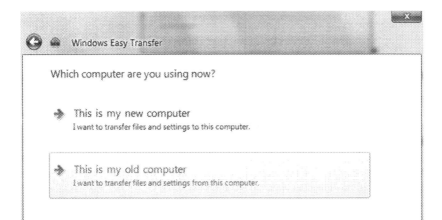

First, select the users whose files you want to transfer to your new machine by clicking the check boxes on the left-hand side, as shown in the following screen.

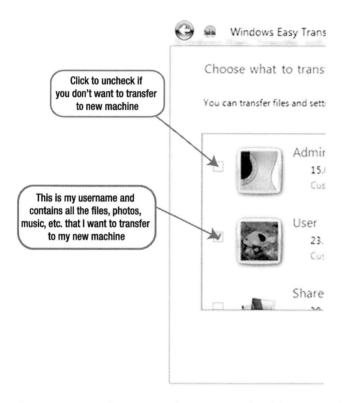

If you are upgrading to Windows 8, you should not transfer any Windows or Program settings, as this can cause compatibility problems.

To remove these options, click on the Customize link under your user name. From the following popup menu, make sure every option is selected except Program Settings and Windows Settings.

Click Next.

In the "Save your files and settings" screen I recommend leaving the password field blank, as adding a password can complicate things later on when you copy the files to your new computer. Click Save.

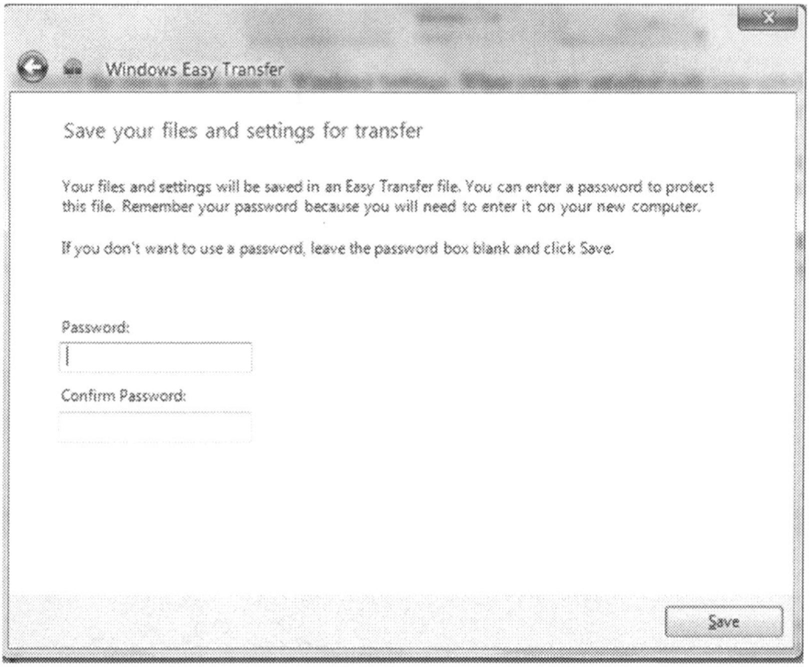

In the next screen, select a location where you wish to save your files. This should be your external hard drive. You will find it listed under the Computer section if you scroll down the left-hand pane of the dialog box.

Click on the drive letter associated with the external drive. In this case it is the Z: drive.

As a guideline, unless you have renamed it, the drive is usually identified by the manufacturer's name. For example, mine is from Data Pacific, so it's called Data. The drive letters are not the same on every machine.

Once you have done that click Save.

Your files will now be saved to the external hard drive, which could take a while.

When the data is saved, click Next to close Windows Easy Transfer. Then unplug your external drive.

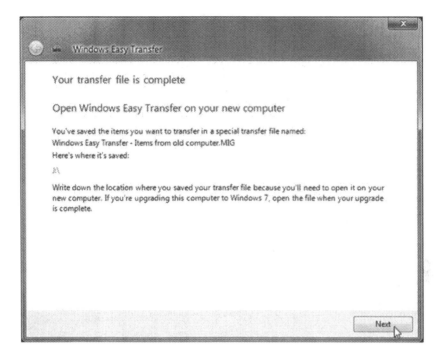

On Your New Computer

Plug your external drive into your new computer.

From the Start screen, click your desktop tile, then click the File Explorer icon on your taskbar at the bottom

In the File Explorer window, go to the This PC heading and look for your external drive. Find and double click on the file "Windows Easy Transfer – Items from old computer.mig."

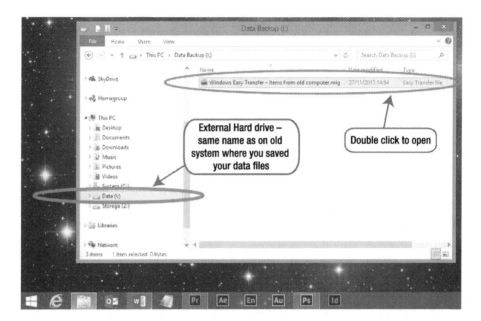

Make sure your user name is checked and then click Transfer.

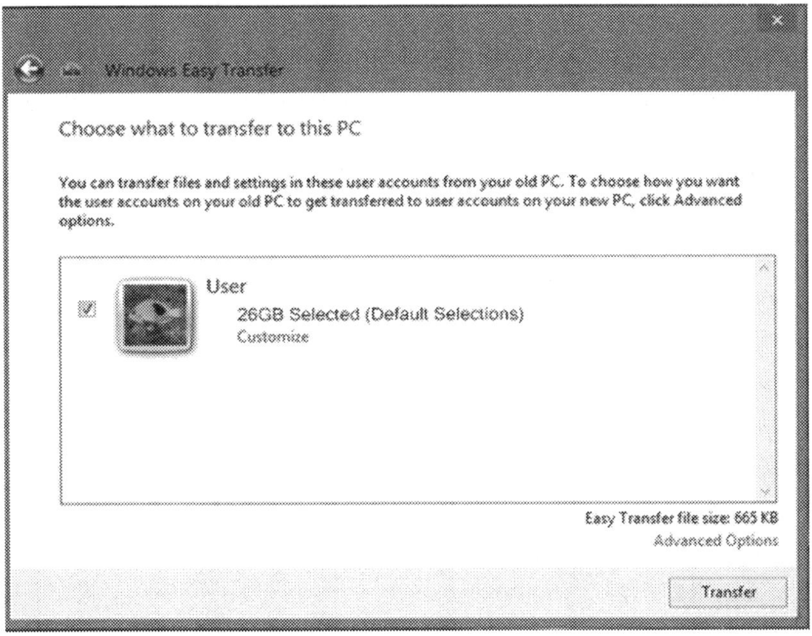

Again, this could take a while. Once your files have finished transferring, you will see the following screen. Click Close.

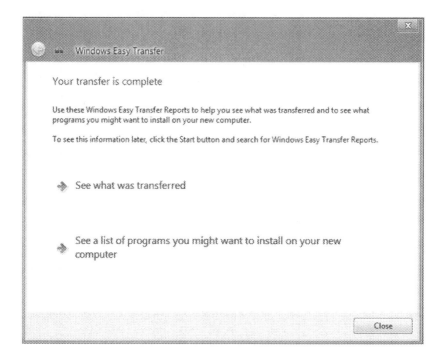

Now that we have our files from our old computer, we can get to know Windows 8 a little better.

■ ■ ■

CHAPTER 2

Getting to Know Windows

The Start Screen

Once you have logged on, you will be greeted with the Start screen. The Start screen is made up of an arrangement of colorful tiles, with each tile representing an application. You click (or tap) the tile to run the app.

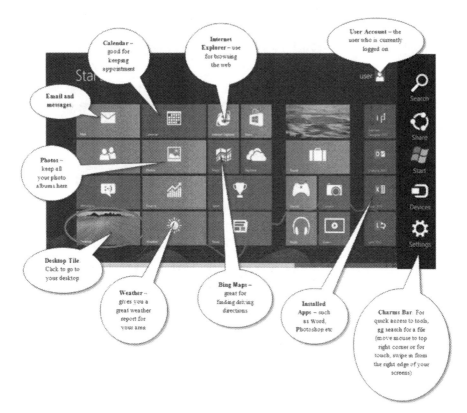

A Closer Look at the Start Screen

You can view all applications by moving your mouse to the bottom of the screen. A small "down" arrow will appear.

The Start screen also has some hidden menus—the Recently Opened Apps menu on the top left reveals all apps that are currently open.

The top-right corner reveals the Charms Bar for settings and options.

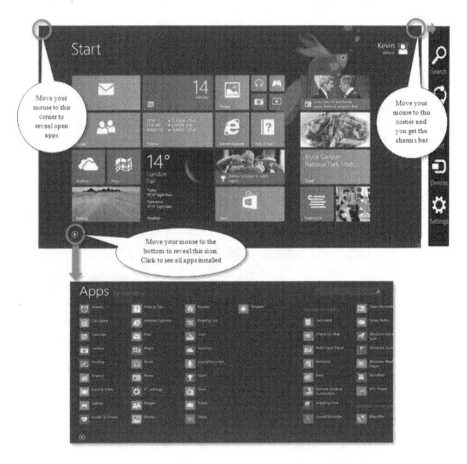

The Desktop

The desktop is where all your apps, such as Microsoft Word and Adobe Photoshop, run and allow you to work.

The desktop hasn't really changed much since the initial release of Windows 8. There are a few tweaks to the Library window (shown here) as well as the addition of a Start button.

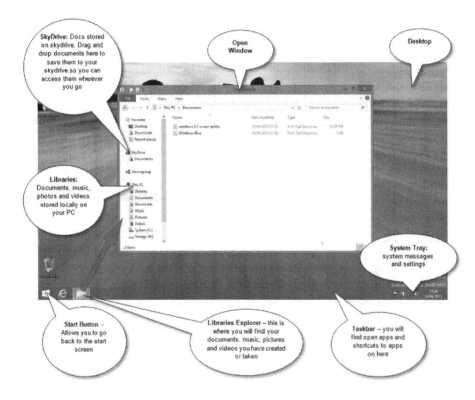

To get back to the Start screen from the desktop, press the Windows key on your keyboard. This is usually in the bottom row. Another option is to click the Start button on the left-hand side of the screen.

For Diehard Desktop Fans

Specifically aimed at point-and-click desktop users, Windows 8.1 allows you to boot directly to the desktop and to change the way the Start screen acts to make it less intrusive.

Here's how. Make your way to your desktop and right click on an empty area of the taskbar, then click Properties. Next select the Navigation tab.

Taskbar and Navigation properties

Taskbar | Navigation | Jump Lists | Toolbars

Corner navigation

☑ When I point to the upper-right corner, show the charms

☑ When I click the upper-left corner, switch between my recent apps

☑ Replace Command Prompt with Windows PowerShell in the menu when I right-click the lower-left corner or press Windows key +X

Start screen

☐ Go to the desktop instead of Start when I sign in

☐ Show my desktop background on Start

☐ Always show Start on my main display when I press the Windows logo key

☐ Show the Apps view au

☐ Search everywhere inst Apps view

☐ List desktop apps first i category

To automatically load up your desktop instead of the start screen when you turn on your computer tick this box

Toolbars ▸
Cascade windows
Show windows stacked
Show windows side by side
Show the desktop

Right click here on taskbar where there are no icons

Task Manager
✔ Lock the taskbar
Properties

OK | Cancel | Apply

Another feature I find useful is "Show the Apps view automatically when I go to start."

If you tick this box, your Start screen will appear as a list of apps. This is useful if you have a lot of applications installed.

The rest of the options on this tab do not provide any real benefit and are best left as they are.

The Taskbar

The taskbar shows applications that are currently open. It can also be used for pinning shortcuts to favorite applications, such as Internet Explorer, for quick access.

On the right-hand side of the taskbar is the area known as the system tray. The system tray contains miniature icons for easy access to system functions such as the printer, volume, clock, and any system messages or alerts. Click on an icon to view and access the details and controls.

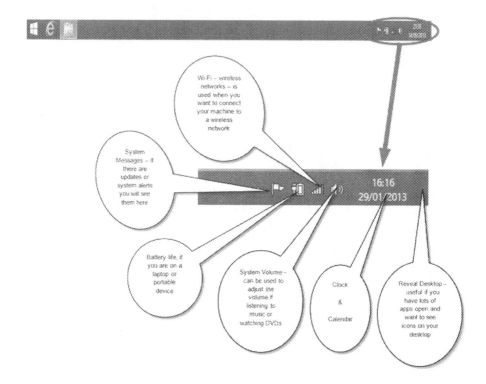

Charms

Charms is a new feature introduced in Windows 8 that gives you access to Search, Share, Start, Devices, and Settings.

Move the mouse to the upper-right corner of your screen to see the charms. When the charms appear, move up or down the edge to click the one you want.

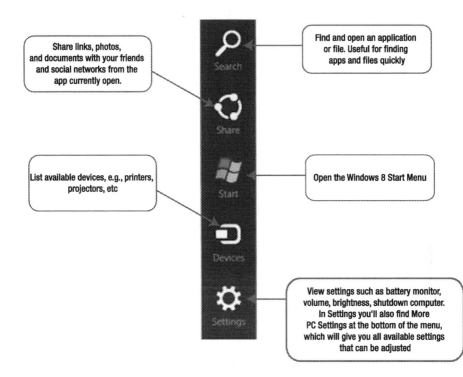

Share links, photos, and documents with your friends and social networks from the app currently open.

Find and open an application or file. Useful for finding apps and files quickly

List available devices, e.g., printers, projectors, etc

Open the Windows 8 Start Menu

View settings such as battery monitor, volume, brightness, shutdown computer. In Settings you'll also find More PC Settings at the bottom of the menu, which will give you all available settings that can be adjusted

The Snap Feature

A feature I find helpful in windows 8 is the ability to snap different applications side by side as you are working. Thus, you could have Microsoft Word running on one side of your screen and Internet Explorer running next to it.

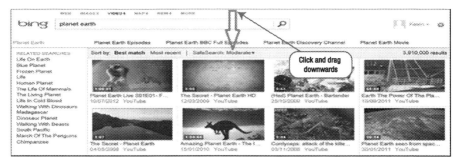

Click and drag downwards

Drag the window to the left-hand side of the screen until the black screen divider appears, then release your mouse.

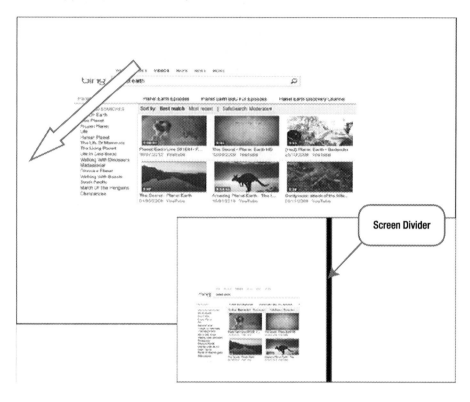

Click your mouse in the very bottom-left corner of the screen to get back to the Start screen, then click on the other application you want. For example, Microsoft Word, as shown in the following screen.

This can be done with any Windows application. It makes working with two different applications easier as you no longer have to toggle between them.

You can see in the following example a bit of research on Planet Earth using online encyclopedias and Microsoft Word side by side.

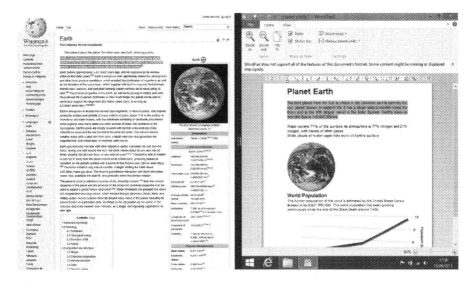

■   ■   ■

CHAPTER 3

Setting Up Users

Adding a New User

On the Start screen activate the Charms Bar and select Settings.

From the Settings charm select "Change PC settings." Then click "Accounts," followed by "Other accounts."

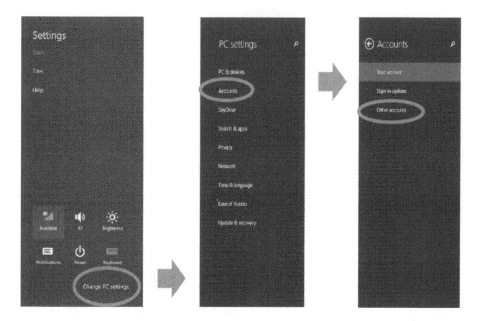

In the screen that appears click "Add an account."

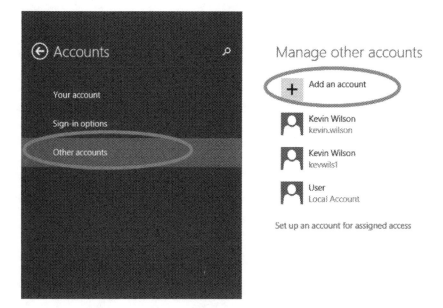

Once on the "Create a Microsoft account" page, enter the required information: first and last name, email address, password, and country/region. Then click Next.

On the "Add security info" page add your date of birth and gender, country code, a phone number (optional at time of writing), and an alternate email address. Then click Next.

Finally, type the random characters displayed on the screen. This is done to stop Internet robots from creating email accounts and sending out unsolicited email. Click Next.

Once the account is confirmed, click Finish.

Set Up a Microsoft Account Online

You can also sign up online if you prefer by going to http://signup.live.com.

Fill out the form and click "I accept."

Where are you from?

Country/region

United Kingdom ⌄

Postal Code

Help us make sure you're not a robot

Enter the characters that you see
New | Audio

PFML6 KSP

☐ Send me emails with promotional offers from Microsoft. (You can unsubscribe at any time.)

Click **I accept** to agree to the Microsoft services agreement and privacy & cookies statement.

I accept

Change to Microsoft Account on Your PC

If you set up your PC without a Microsoft account, you can change it to either a Microsoft account or a local account.

A Microsoft account is set up on Microsoft's servers and allows you access to SkyDrive, email, Microsoft Office, and the app store. A local account is only accessible on your PC—and nowhere else—so you wouldn't be able to use SkyDrive or email on another computer.

To set up your Microsoft account, activate the Charms Bar by moving your mouse to the top right corner of your screen. Click Settings.

On the screen that appears, click "Change PC settings," as in shown the following pane on the left.

In the middle pane, click Accounts, then click "Your account" in the right pane.

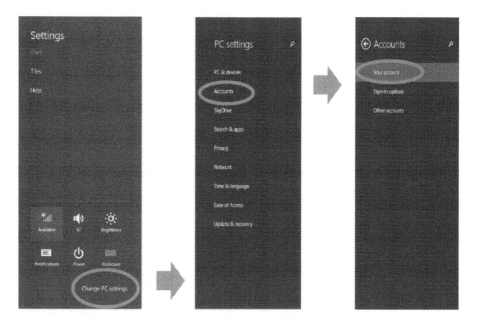

Then click "Connect to a Microsoft account" in the following screen.

In the "Sign in with a Microsoft account" dialog box, type in your Windows Live ID and Gmail, Yahoo, or Hotmail email address, and then click Next.

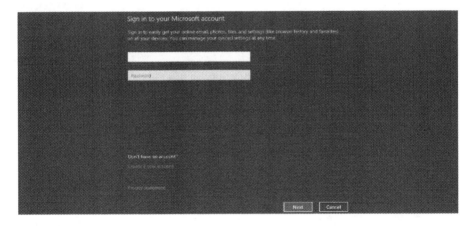

■ Note: If you don't have a Microsoft account already, tap or click "Don't have an account?" and then follow the instructions. Or sign up online if you prefer (see "Setting Up Microsoft Account Online" section).

As a security precaution, you will be asked for a security code, which will be emailed to the email address you used when you created your Microsoft account, as shown in the following screen.

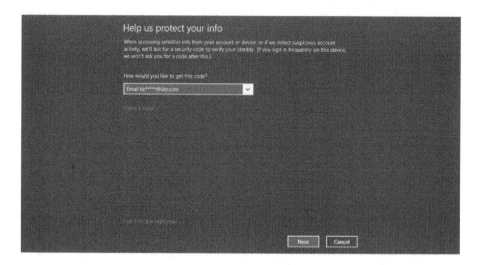

Click Next. This will send an email to your address.

Go check your email and copy the code. The email will look like the following message.

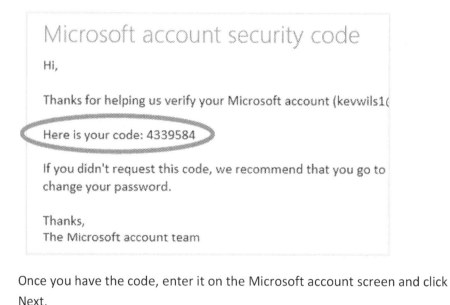

Once you have the code, enter it on the Microsoft account screen and click Next.

Click Next until you're done. You can now log in with the email address and password you entered in the above procedure.

CHAPTER 4

Setting Up Printers

Printers come in all different types, sizes, and makes. It isn't possible to cover them all in this guide, but I will attempt to go over the basics that seem to work for most printers.

There are essentially two types of printers: laser and inkjet.

Laser Printers

A laser printer uses a laser to project an image of the page to be printed onto an electrically charged rotating drum. The drum is then coated in toner and burned onto the page. These printers are usually used for high-speed printing of high-quality documents.

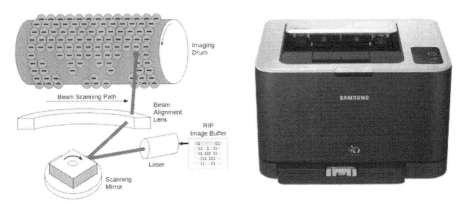

The laser printer uses toner cartridges for black and three color cartridges, one for each primary color (yellow, cyan, and magenta). These cartridges can be expensive. Laser printers are good if you do a lot of printing, such as if you run a business, have an office full of computers, or have a large family that all want to print things out from their laptops.

Inkjet Printers

Inkjet printers create a digital image by firing droplets of ink onto paper.

These printers can be good for everyday use for printing short documents or a photograph on photopaper.

These printers use a black ink cartridge and a color cartridge and are usually aimed at home users. They are cheaper than laser printers and are good if you want to print photographs, a letter, and so forth.

Installation

Most printers connect to your computer using USB. Setup isn't always the same for each printer, so referring to the setup instructions that come with the printer is a good idea.

To set up printers in Windows 8, insert the setup disk that comes with the printer into your DVD drive; the disk should run and guide you through the process.

I found it best to install the setup disk first, then connect the printer to the USB port.

Accessing Installed Printers

Printing from desktop applications in Windows 8, such as Microsoft Word, works the same as it did in previous versions of Windows, so there is no need to detail it here. However, printing from Windows 8 Metro apps is a little different than in earlier version of Windows, although the process works fine once you get used to it. Let's look at that now. From the Charms Bar, move your mouse pointer to the top-right corner of the screen and select Devices.

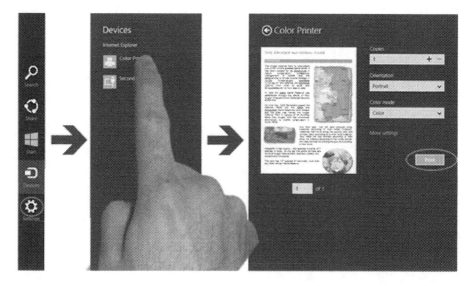

Select your printer from the list. Click on the name of the printer that you wish to use.

From the selected printer's Settings screen you can change the various settings, such as number of copies and orientation. Click the Print button to print.

■ ■ ■

CHAPTER 5

Setting Up Internet

There are two main types of Internet connection: ADSL and Cable. ADSL, or digital subscriber line (DSL), enables fast data transmission over copper telephone lines. Cable Internet provides Internet access using coaxial cable. Most cable companies offer this with their television subscriptions.

ADSL

Nowadays, most computers access the Internet using Wi-Fi (wireless Internet). To use Wi-Fi you'll need to sign up with an Internet service provider (ISP), such as AT&T. Typically the ISP will send you a router, as shown in the following picture.

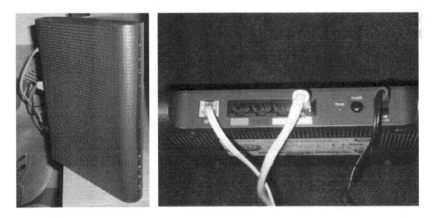

This usually plugs into your phone line using a filter. This type of connection to the Internet over the phone line is known as ADSL.

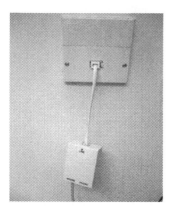

Cable Internet

Cable Internet provides Internet access using coaxial cable, which was developed to carry television signals, instead of copper telephone cables, which are used in ADSL. All cable subscribers in a neighborhood connect to a cable company's central office.

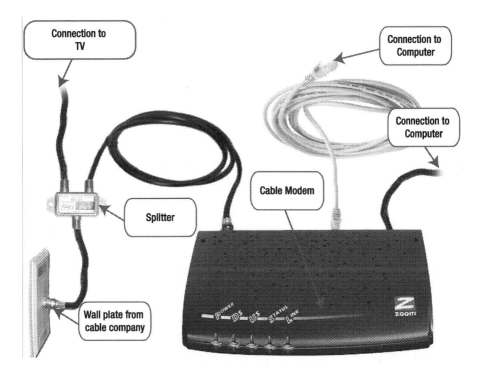

Following is an image of the back of a cable modem. Your computer connects to the modem using the Ethernet port via an Ethernet cable. Your Internet connection from the cable company connects to the cable port.

A lot of companies offer broadband Internet access with their TV packages. They send you a cable modem that provides Wi-Fi access in addition to a "hard-connection" option via the USB port.

Setting Up Wi-Fi on Your Computer

The router or modem has a code on the side that you enter into your computer to access the Internet.

If your modem is hard wired, just plug the Ethernet cable into your laptop; you don't need to set up the Wi-Fi unless your cable modem has Wi-Fi capability.

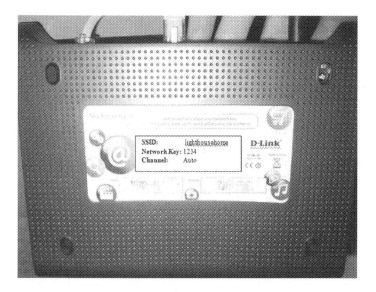

The SSID is the name of your network. This will have been preset by your ISP. The Network Key is a password that is used to secure your network so no one else nearby can access your Wi-Fi.

Once your router is set up and plugged in, and your ISP has given you the green light, you can connect your computer to your Wi-Fi.

Activate the Charms Bar and click Settings.

Click the Wi-Fi icon, which is circled in the following screen.

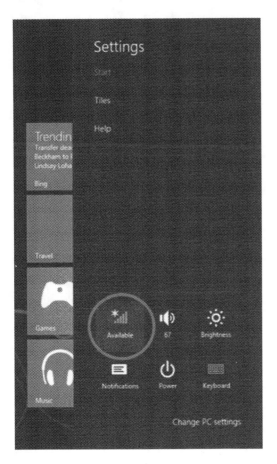

This displays all the SSIDs of nearby Wi-Fi routers. Select the one that matches the SSID on the back of your router, making sure Connect Automatically is selected, then click Connect.

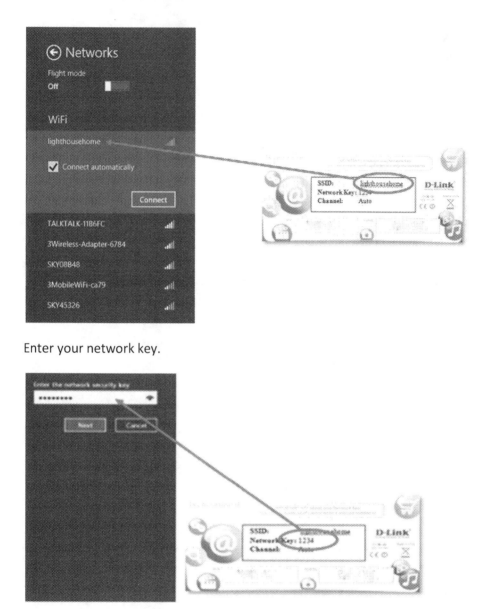

Enter your network key.

If you are having problems, contact your ISP tech support line. The details should be in the package they sent to you.

You are now ready to browse the Internet.

CHAPTER 6

■ ■ ■

Common Tasks

Finding Applications

Most common applications can be found on the Start screen.

Move your mouse to the very bottom of the screen until the downward pointing arrow appears, then click on it to reveal all the installed applications on your computer.

A quick way to find applications is to activate the Charms Bar by moving your mouse to the top right-hand corner of the screen. Then, in the bar that appears, click Search.

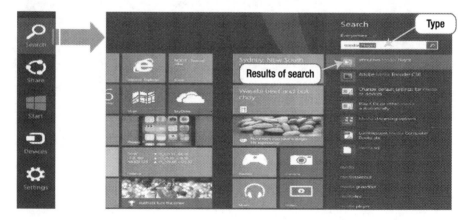

You can search different types of things on your computer; for example, applications such as Word or Media Player, Disk Defragment, or Windows Update. You can also search for more specific things, such as documents, letters, photos, and so on by clicking the dropdown box that says Everything and changing it to Settings.

Finding Files

There are a number of different ways you can find your files in Windows 8. You can use the search feature or you can browse through your files on the desktop.

Searching for Files

On your Start screen, type in the name of the file you are looking for. Windows will return search results down the right-hand side.

Files in Desktop

You can also find files when you are on your desktop using File Explorer. To open File Explorer, click the icon on the bottom left of the following screen.

Notice the Libraries folder in the window that appears (circled in the lower left-hand side). Your libraries will be grouped into subfolders: Documents, Music, Pictures, and Videos. It's good practice to save your files in the appropriate folders. For example, Word documents in the Documents folder, pictures and photos in the Pictures folder, etc.

Quick Search the Internet

You can even use the search tool on the Charms Bar to search using the Bing search engine. For example, if I wanted to find websites and images about computers, I would type "computer" into the search box. At the bottom right of the following screen you will see some suggested web searches. Click on the one that closely matches your search query.

If you scroll across your screen, you will see a list of images and websites for your keyword search.

This makes using Windows 8 on a touch screen easier.

Burning CD/DVDs

Insert a blank DVD or CD and select "With a CD/DVD player."

Once you have set up your disk, drag the files and folders you want to burn to the disk to the DVD drive in your File Explorer window.

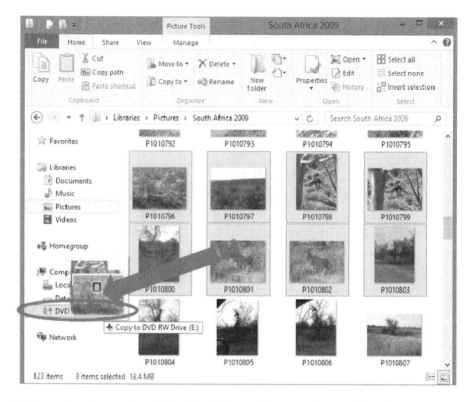

To burn the data to the disk, right click on the DVD drive in the File Explorer window and select "Burn to disc" from the menu.

Burning Audio CDs

Burning audio CDs can be done from media player. From the Charms Bar go to Search and type "media."

Once in Media Player click on the Burn tab. You can now click and drag tracks to the Burn tab to create a playlist.

Once your disk is full or you have the number of tracks you want, click Start Burn to create your CD.

Scanning Documents

By default Windows uses Windows Fax and Scan to scan documents. There are other apps available that are bundled with scanners and available for purchase, but for simplicity I am going to use Windows Fax and Scan. Activate the Charms Bar, go to Search, and type "scan."

Click Windows Fax and Scan, and you should see the main screen.

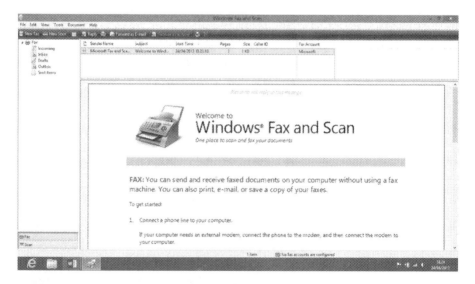

Plug your scanner in. If this is the first time, Windows 8 will try to automatically install it.

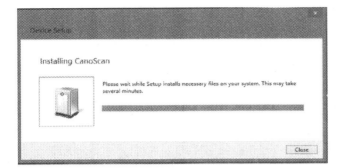

If it fails to install, run the software that comes with the scanner; see the manufacturer's website for more information. To scan a document, click New Scan.

You will find all your scans in your Scanned Documents folder in your Documents library. This can be accessed from your desktop.

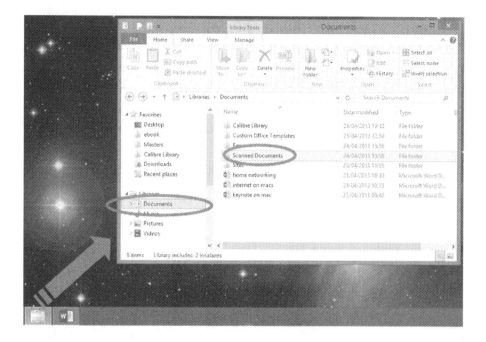

Printing Documents

There is a difference between printing from Metro apps and Windows 8 applications. Let's review both now.

Printing in Windows 8 Metro

Printing from Windows 8 Metro apps are a little different than Windows 8, but the process works fine once you get used to it. From within the application you want to print from (in this example I want to print a web page from Internet Explorer), activate the Charms Bar by moving your mouse pointer to the top right corner of the screen and select Devices.

Select your printer from the list. Click on the name of the printer that you wish to use. A settings screen for your printer appears, where you can change the number of copies, print orientation, color mode, and other settings.

Click on the Print button to print.

Printing in Windows 8

Printing from desktop Windows 8 applications, such as Word, works the same as it does in previous versions of Windows.

File -> Print

Uploading Files from Digital Cameras

Plug in your camera using the USB cable. As soon as you plug in for the first time, a message will appear on the top right of the screen asking you what to do with the device you have just plugged in. Tap or click it.

Once you click on it, click "Import photos and videos."

Choose what to do with this device.

 Copy pictures to your computer
Picasa3

 Import photos and videos
Photos

 Open device to view files
File Explorer

 Take no action

Note: You will only have to do this the first time you plug your camera into your computer. When you plug your camera in again you will go straight to the photo app.

Select the photos you want by clicking on them, then type in the name of the album in which you want to group your photos. This could be Wedding or Birthday. Then click Import.

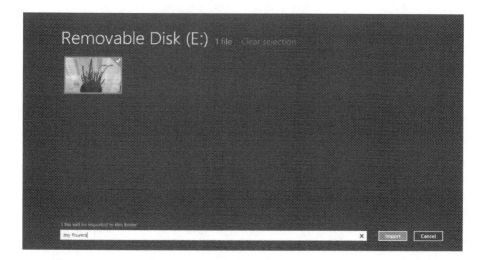

Once you are done importing, click Open Folder. Here you will be able to see the photos you just imported.

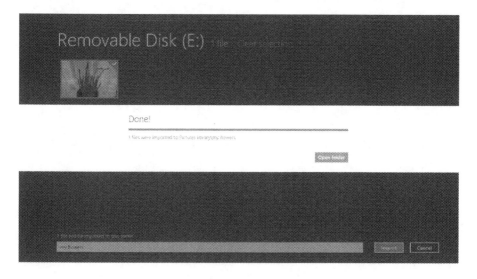

To access your photos at any time, click Photos app on the Start screen.

Maps

Activate the Charms Bar and select Search. In the search field type the place you are looking for. Make sure you click Maps to tell Windows to search in Bing Maps.

Right click on the map to reveal the options bar. On map style you can select street map or satellite map (aerial view). I find the aerial view to be more descriptive when finding directions.

Right click on the map and select Directions. Enter your current location and destination.

Hit Enter, and Bing Maps will bring up a route, shown at the top of the screen and indicated by a blue line on the map.

Calendar

To access Calendar click on it from the Start screen.

Once Calendar has started, it will show you the current month; it also shows public holidays.

To add an appointment, double click on the day in the month and fill in the fields as shown below. Then click Save when done.

To move to previous or next month, move your pointer over to the top left or right to reveal the arrows

Using Internet Explorer

On your Start screen tap or click Internet Explorer.

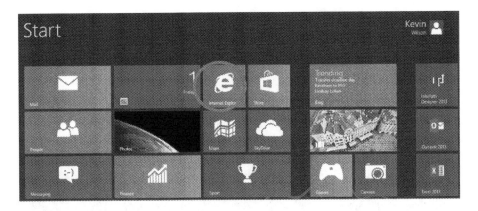

In the URL address bar below, type the name of the thing you are looking for. For example, I'm looking for the Amazon website. So I will type "Amazon" into the address bar.

As you start to type, Internet Explorer will try to find the website. You can see below that Internet Explorer has found Amazon's website. Just click or tap on the result, and it will take you to the website.

When browsing the web, Internet Explorer may hide your address bar. You can get it back by clicking on the three dots on the bottom right of the screen, circled below.

Adding a Site to Favorites

To add the site to Favorites, find your address bar by clicking on the three dots on the bottom right-hand side of the previous screen. Internet Explorer hides this bar when you are not using it.

Click the star icon, shown in the following screen. This will reveal your Favorites panel.

Then click the Add to Favorites icon, circled in the following screen.

In the popup box that appears, give your favorite a name, then click Add.

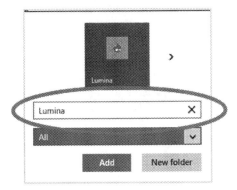

You can access your Favorites by clicking the three dots on the bottom right of your screen to reveal the address bar.

Then click a favorite site (circled below) to go straight to the website.

Using Email

When you first set up an account in Windows 8 you'll be offered the chance to log in with your Windows Live ID. If you don't have one, it's worth setting one up.

From the Start screen, click on the Mail icon.

The left pane in the following screen shows your account's inbox, drafts, and so on. The middle pane shows a list of messages corresponding to the box selected in the left-hand pane. The right pane displays the full email message that you selected in the middle pane.

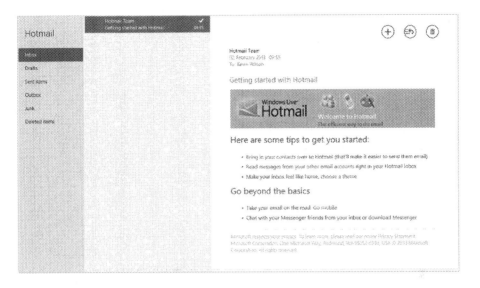

If you want to add other email accounts—perhaps you have a Google mail or Yahoo mail account—you can do this.

You can add a new account with the Settings charm. Sweep a finger inwards from the right side of the screen or move the mouse pointer to the top right corner of the screen. Then choose Settings.

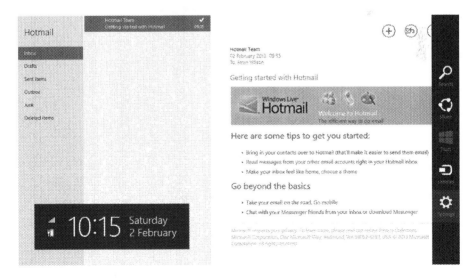

Next, choose Accounts.

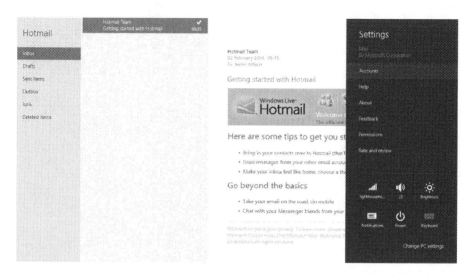

A new pane will appear. Tap or click Add an Account and enter the details for a new email account.

Pick the account type. You can choose between Hotmail, Google, Yahoo, and Exchange, depending on the type of email you want.

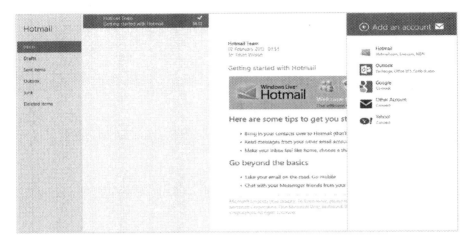

Now just type in your email address and password for the account you want to add and click Connect. You can repeat this process to add more accounts.

If you want to delete an account, just tap and hold, or click and hold on it, and a Delete option will appear.

Sending an Email

To send a new email message click Send New Message.

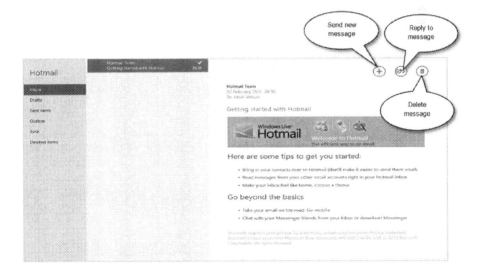

Fill in the email address and type your message. Once you are done, click Send Message.

Family Safety

Keeping your kids safe while using the Internet is an ongoing concern for parents. With Windows 8, you can monitor what your kids are doing, no matter where they use their PC. To do this you have to create a Windows user account for each child and check the box to turn on Family Safety.

This enables parents to review weekly reports that tell you what your child is up to. You'll also be able to make sure children aren't associating with online predators.

After creating a new account with Family Safety turned on, you'll automatically be taken to the Family Safety setup section in the Control Panel.

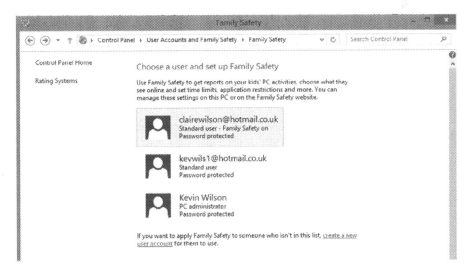

Click on the user account you want to configure.

On the Configure screen you can select settings to filter and monitor web activity, set time limits, and even restrict which applications the user can access.

So, for example, homework hour could allow use of Microsoft Office apps such as Word and not allow use of Internet, email, etc.

Web filtering allows you to restrict websites and downloads. You can allow or block specific websites. You can filter websites by enabling the strict mode for SafeSearch, which filters out adult content from search engines such as Google.

Time limits allow you to set a time allowances.

Windows Store and game restrictions allows you to control which apps and games the user can use based on Entertainment Software Rating Board ratings, or you can block certain games specifically.

App restrictions lets you control which apps and programs the user can use.

Using SkyDrive

SkyDrive, not to be confused with SkyDrive Pro, is a free file-hosting service that allows users to upload and sync files to cloud storage and then access them from a web browser. It also allows users to keep the files private, share them with contacts, or make the files public. Publicly shared files do not require a Microsoft account to access.

To access your SkyDrive in a web browser go to:

skydrive.live.com

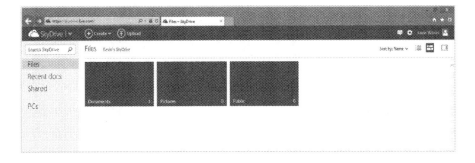

Once logged on you can access documents, pictures, and your public area.

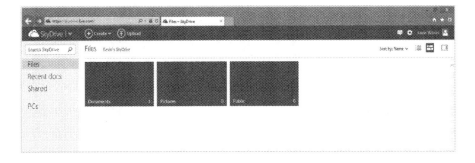

In your documents area you can actually use a web-based version of Microsoft Word 2013 to edit your document and save it back to your SkyDrive.

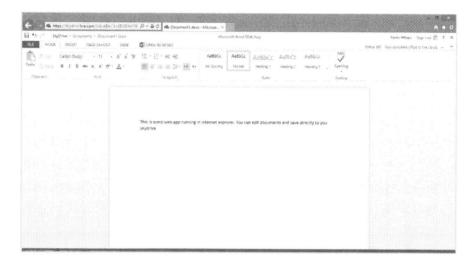

If you are using Windows 8, you can access these files and upload others to SkyDrive by using the SkyDrive app on your Start screen.

Click in the documents section to find your files.

When you open them up they will load directly into your installation of Microsoft Word 2013.

If Word asks you to log in, enter your Microsoft Account email address and password.

Saving onto SkyDrive is the same as if you were saving the file to your computer. Just select SkyDrive from the options in the Save As screen in Office.

Organizing Your Music

Music app links in with your Windows account so you can buy any albums or tracks you want.

The Music app also automatically scans your computer for any music and adds it to your Music library.

Buying Songs and Albums

You can buy songs or albums by your favorite artist right from the Music app.

To buy an album or song, type the name of the artist into the search field on the left-hand side of the screen. Click Full Catalogue to view all the albums in the music store that correspond with your search term.

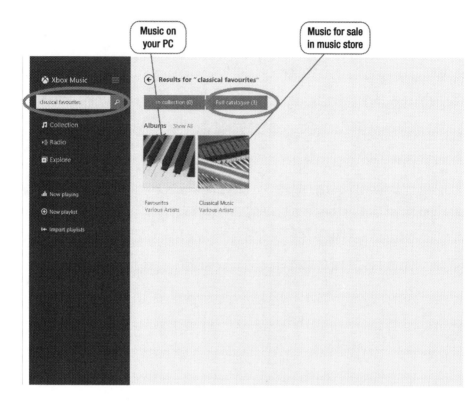

To buy any of the albums, click on an album cover. Then in the screen that appears, click "Buy album for...," as shown circled in the screen.

The album songs will download to your computer to the Collection folder, located on the left-hand side of the screen.

Playing Music

To access your songs, click Collection. This lists all the albums on your computer. Then double click one of the album covers on the right.

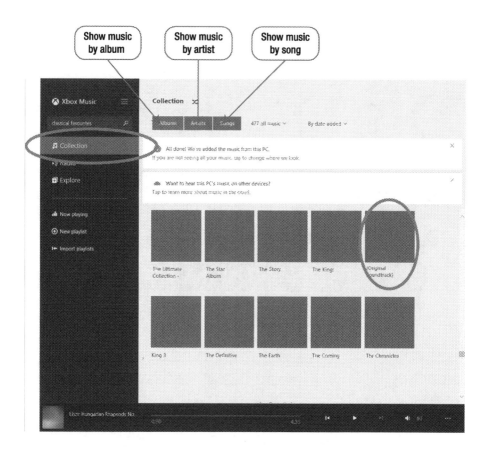

To play the album, click the Play icon circled the following screen. Or to play a specific track, double click the track name.

Copying Songs from a CD to Your PC

If you want to copy music from a CD onto your computer, use Windows Media Player. Open the Search charm.

Enter Windows Media Player into the search field and then tap or click Windows Media Player in the results on the left-hand side.

Insert an audio CD into the CD drive. Select the check boxes next to the songs you want to rip, and then tap or click Rip CD.

When your songs have been copied, you can find and play them in the Music app.

Videos and DVDs

You can watch movies, TV programs, and other videos on your computer. Some are free and some you must pay for. You can buy movies or rent them and have them streamed directly to your computer.

To go to the movie store click Video on the Start screen.

You can browse the store or, if you are searching for a specific genre or movie/TV show title, click the Search icon and type in your desired title, as shown below.

In the search field that appears, enter the film title or TV program you are looking for.

Search for movies, TV shows, or your own videos

To buy, rent, or watch them just click the image. From here click Rent to watch the entire movie or click Play Trailer to watch just the trailer.

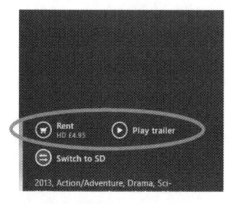

Playing DVDs

If you like watching DVDs on your PC, you'll have to download a free player as Windows 8 can't play DVD videos out of the box. The best-supported player is VLC Media Player, which plays back DVDs and CDs along with a range of other file types.

Just go to their website and click Download: www.videolan.org.

When prompted with your download, click Run and follow the instructions.

Using Microsoft App Store

The app store allows you to download and install apps. It has both free and paid apps.

Opening App Store

You can start the app store by clicking or tapping the tile on the Start screen.

Once the store opens, you can browse through the top paid apps, top free apps, or new releases, or, if you are searching for a specific app, activate your Charms Bar and select Search.

Browse the App Store

On the main screen you can scroll left and right to view the top-rated apps in different categories, such as entertainment, photos, music, sports, news, etc.

These are broken down into sections for the top 100 apps you have to pay for, top 100 free apps, and apps that have just been released.

Search the App Store

If you are searching for a specific app, activate the Charms Bar and select Search.

In the search field, enter a word describing the type of app you are looking for. In this example, I am looking for graphics apps to edit my photographs.

Search

Store

graphics

Apps

Settings

Files

Music

Bing

Finance

Games

Internet Explorer

To see details on the app, click its icon.

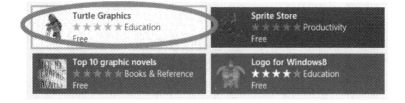

From here you will see a write up describing the app, the price, and some screen shots so you can see what the app looks like.

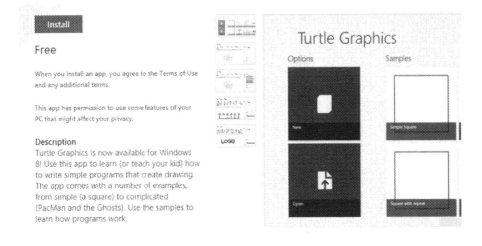

Downloading an App

To download an app, select the app you want; in this example I am going to download Google Search from the top 100 free apps.

After selecting the app you want, the app store will show you the app details screen telling you about the app with descriptions, system requirements, and reviews.

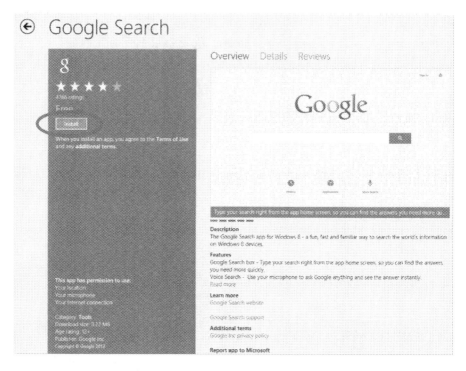

Click the Install button. You may be asked for your Microsoft Account email and password.

Once the app is installed it will appear on your Start screen.

Click the app icon to run the app.

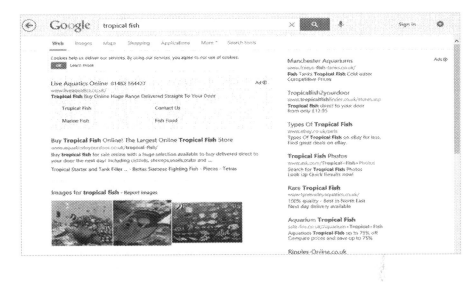

Connecting to Projectors

Open the Charms Bar, select Devices, then click Second Screen.

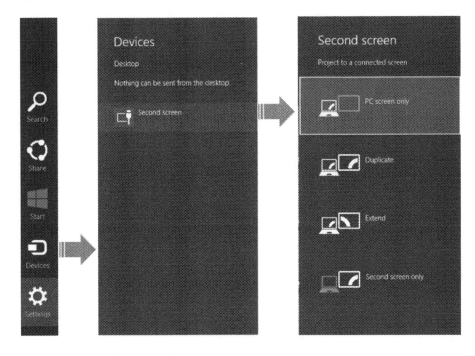

From there, you have the following options:

- PC Screen Only. This disables the projector so the information is only seen on the PC's monitor.

- Duplicate PC Screen on Projector. Everything you do on the monitor will be duplicated on the projected screen.

- Extend PC Screen onto Projector. The projector acts as an extension of your PC screen rather than just a duplicate. This allows you to move windows from the PC's screen to the projector screen and vice versa.

- Second Screen Only. This disables the PC's monitor so the display only appears on the projected screen.

Keyboard Shortcuts

Windows 8 was designed with both tablet and PC users in mind. While touchscreen users can swipe and tap their way through the new interface, those who prefer the traditional PC setup might find the system a bit awkward to navigate. Fortunately, keyboard shortcuts make it a bit easier to navigate without a touch screen.

To close an app, hold down Alt, press F4.

To get back to the Start screen, press the Windows key.

Here are some common shortcuts to keep in mind:

⊞ + start typing	Search your PC
Ctrl plus ('+') or Ctrl minus ('-')	Zoom in or out of a large number of items
Ctrl + Scroll wheel	Zoom in or out of a large number of items
⊞ + C	Open the charms menu
⊞ + F	Open the Search charm to search files
⊞ + H	Open the Share charm
⊞ + I	Open the Settings charm
⊞ + J	Switch the main app and snapped app
⊞ + K	Open the Devices charm
⊞ + O	Lock the screen orientation
⊞ + Q	Open the Search charm to search apps
⊞ + W	Open the Search charm to search settings
⊞ + Z	Show the commands available in the app
⊞ + spacebar	Switch input language and keyboard layout
⊞ + Ctrl + spacebar	Change to previously selected input
⊞ + Tab	Cycle through open apps
⊞ + Ctrl + Tab	Cycle through open apps and snap them as they are cycled
⊞ + Shift + Tab	Cycle through open apps in reverse order
⊞ + Pg Up	Move the Start screen and apps to the monitor on the left
⊞ + Pg Dn	Move the Start screen and apps to the monitor on the right
⊞ + Shift + Period ('.')	Snaps apps to the left
⊞ + Period ('.')	Snaps apps to the right
Esc	Stop or exit the current task

⊞ + L	Lock your PC or switch users
⊞ + M	Minimize all windows
⊞ + Shift + M	Restore minimized windows on the desktop
⊞ + P	Choose a presentation display mood
⊞ + R	Open the Run dialogue box
⊞ + T	Cycle through apps on the taskbar
⊞ + V	Cycle through notifications
⊞ + Shift + V	Cycle through notifications in reverse order
⊞ + X	Open the Quick Link menu
⊞ + F1	Open Windows Help and Support
⊞ + Up arrow	Maximize the desktop window
⊞ + Down arrow	Minimize the desktop window
⊞ + plus ("+") or minus ("-")	Zoom in or out using Magnifier
Alt + F4	Close the active item, or exit the active app
Alt + Enter	Display properties for the selected item
Control + C	Copy the selected item
Control + X	Cut the selected item
Control + V	Paste the selected item
Control + Y	Redo an action
Control + Z	Undo an action
F1	Display Help
F2	Rename the selected item
F3	Search for a file or folder
F4	Display the address bar list in the File Explorer
F5	Refresh the active window

Hot Corners

Windows 8 makes use of what it calls hotspots. These can be accessed by moving the pointer to various corners of the screen to reveal certain tools.

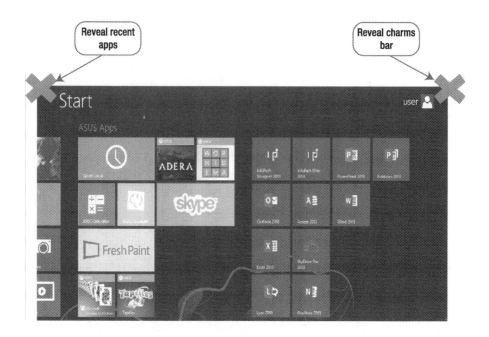

CHAPTER 7

■ ■ ■

Computer Maintenance

Regular computer maintenance will extend its life. Let's review some of the better options available and practices to adhere to.

Anti-Virus Software

A lot of this software comes pre-installed on the machine you buy and is offered on a subscription basis, so you have to pay to update the software.

Buying this software for home computers isn't necessary these days, as there are options available on the Internet that are just as good. Plus Windows 8 comes with its own version of anti-virus protection called Windows Defender. Microsoft Security Essentials is another option and is free to download and use on a home computer. Note that if you are running Windows 8, you don't need to install Security Essentials.

Open your web browser and go to the Security Essentials website:

www.microsoft.com/en-gb/security/pc-security/mse.aspx

There you can download and run the installation. Simply follow the instructions on screen.

When you click Download you will get a prompt similar to the one below; make sure you click Run.

Then follow the instructions on the screen.

Backing Up

If you have ever lost data because of a computer glitch or crash, you know how frustrating it can be. We all need a good backup strategy. I'm going to go through the strategy that has worked well for me over the years.

First of all, go buy yourself a good external hard disk. This is a small device that plugs into a USB port on your computer. The following image shows a typical specification for an external hard disk.

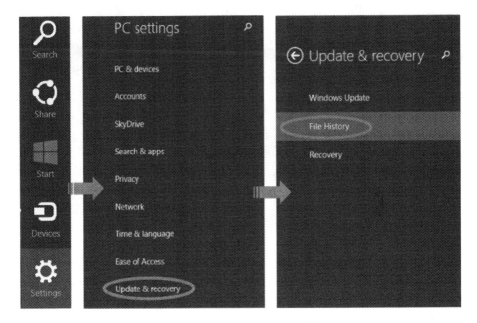

Plug your external drive into an open USB port. Activate Charms Bar, select PC Settings, and click Update & Recovery. Then select File History.

To activate file history click "Select a drive," shown in the screen below. Make sure you have your external drive plugged in.

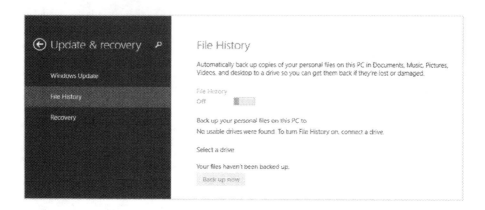

Restore Files

To restore files click Restore Personal Files. Go to your desktop and activate the Charms Bar, then select Control Panel. Select "Save backup copies of your files with File History."

Click Restore Personal Files on the left-hand side of the window that appears. Use the left and right arrows at the bottom to navigate to the date backed up when you know your file was still okay.

Then, in the library section, double click on the folder the file was in (e.g., Pictures if you lost a photo).

Select the photo and, to restore it, click the green button at the bottom of the window.

Flash Drives and Memory Sticks

Also as an extra line of defense, important files can be saved onto a flash drive or memory stick like any of the ones shown here.

These devices don't hold as much data as an external hard disk but can be useful to hold important documents or photos. They can hold 1GB to 64GB.

These devices are also great for moving files to another computer. For example, if you have a photograph or document you want to load onto a friend's computer.

Windows Update

Windows Update usually automatically downloads and installs all updates available for Windows.

Click Check Now to force Windows to update. Or you can click View Details to see what updates have already been installed.

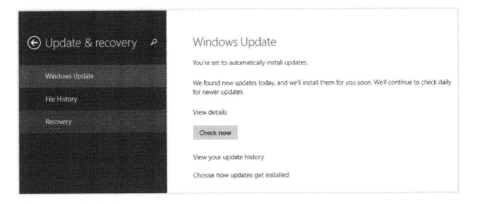

This automatic installation can sometimes be a nuisance if you are working and Windows wants to download and install updates, so I set it to manual install so I can decide when to install updates. If you don't want to worry about it, I would leave it on auto.

If you want to change the settings, go to your desktop, activate the Charms Bar, and select Control Panel. Select System and Security, then select "Turn automatic updating on or off."

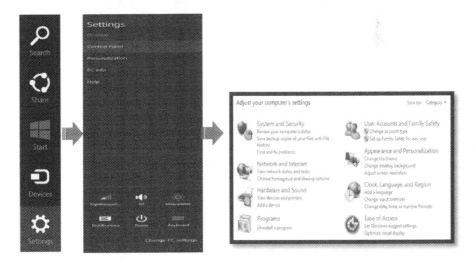

To prevent Windows from automatically installing updates, select "Download updates but let me choose whether to install them."

Important updates

Check for updates but let me choose whether to download and install them   ⌄

Install updates automatically (recommended)
Download updates but let me choose whether to install them
Recomm Check for updates but let me choose whether to download and install them
Never check for updates (not recommended)

Windows will now download all available updates, but it will ask you when it's convenient to install them.

Disk Defragmentation

Data is saved in blocks, called clusters, on the surface of the disk. When a computer saves your file, it writes the data to the next empty cluster on the disk, even if the clusters are not adjacent. This allows faster performance, and usually the disk is spinning fast enough that this has little effect on the time it takes to open the file.

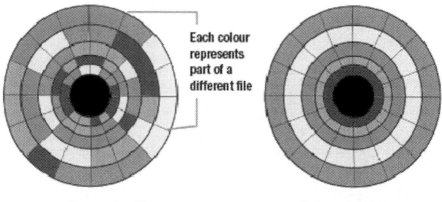

Each colour represents part of a different file

Fragmented Files   Defragmented Files

However, as more and more files are created, saved, deleted, or changed, the data becomes fragmented across the surface of a disk, and it takes longer to access. This can cause problems when launching software (because it will often load many different files as it launches), so bad fragmentation just makes every operation on the computer take longer. Eventually, fragmentation can cause applications to crash, hang, or even corrupt the data.

To defragment the disk in Windows 8, activate Search and type "defragment." Make sure you click Settings to tell Windows to search in the system apps, as shown in the following screen.

Select the drive your system is installed on; this is usually C. Click Optimize.

This will start defragmenting your disk.

Manually Checking Hard Drive for Errors

In Windows 8, Microsoft changed the way we fix corruptions so as to minimize the downtime due to disk checks.

A new file system was introduced, called ReFS, which does not require a manual disk check to repair corruptions.

From the desktop click the File Explorer icon on the taskbar, right click on Local Disk, click Properties, select Tools tab, click Check, then click Scan Drive.

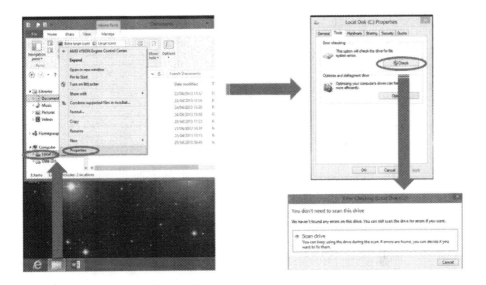

Disk Clean-Up

Over time, Windows gets clogged up with temporary files from browsing the Internet, installing and un-installing software, and general everyday usage.

Open up Search and type "cleanup," making sure you select Settings to tell Windows to search in System Utilities. Click "Free up disk space by deleting unnecessary files."

In the window that appears, you can see a list of all the different files and caches. It is safe to select all these for clearing. Once you are done, click OK, and Windows will clear out all those old files.

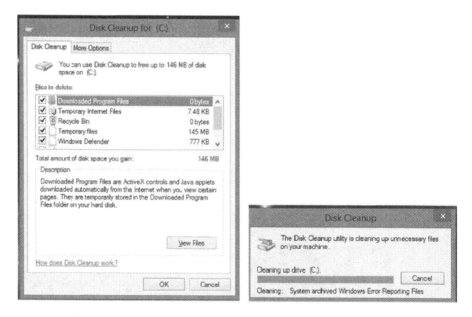

Automatic Maintenance

Windows 8 introduces a new feature that allows you to schedule and run Automatic Maintenance on your computer, such as security updating and scanning, Windows software updates, disk defragmentation, disk volume errors, system diagnostics, etc.

Start-Up Programs

Hit control-alt-delete on your keyboard and select Task Manager from the menu.

Click More Details if you don't see the following screen. Click on the Startup tab. Most of these programs can be disabled with the exception of your sound, video, and network devices.

Name	Publisher	Status	Startup impact
NVIDIA nView Wizard, Versio...	NVIDIA Corporation	Enabled	Medium
CodeMeter Control Center (2)	WIBU-SYSTEMS AG	Enabled	High
iTunesHelper	Apple Inc.	Disabled	None
Program		Disabled	None
Updater	Web Solution Mart	Disabled	None
DivX Update		Disabled	None
QuickFinder Index Scheduler	Corel Corporation	Disabled	None
QuickTime Task	Apple Inc.	Disabled	None
Apple Push	Apple Inc.	Disabled	None
AcroTray	Adobe Systems Inc.	Disabled	None
Adobe Acrobat SpeedLaunc...	Adobe Systems Incorpor...	Disabled	None
Adobe Reader and Acrobat ...	Adobe Systems Incorpor...	Disabled	None
Adobe CS6 Service Manager	Adobe Systems Incorpor...	Disabled	None
SwitchBoard Server (32 bit)	Adobe Systems Incorpor...	Disabled	None
Program		Disabled	None
Microsoft Lync	Microsoft Corporation	Disabled	None

You will also see the startup impact, which shows how much the program slows the machine down. These are the programs that show up in your system tray on the bottom right-hand side of your screen. As you can see below, this system is quite clean—only essential icons appear in the tray.

System Recovery

Windows 8.1 has a feature called Update & Recovery to help you maintain your machine and recover your system if it should fail.

From your Charms Bar, select Settings and Change Computer Settings. Then click Update & Recovery, as shown below.

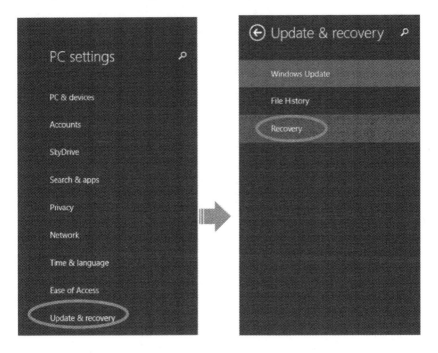

From the screen that appears you can choose a number of options, mainly the first two.

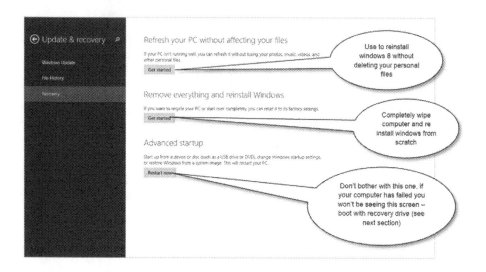

Create a Recovery Drive

To create a recovery drive go to your desktop and activate the Charms Bar, then select Control Panel. From Control Panel select "Save backup copies of your files with file history," and in the window that appears click Recovery on the bottom left.

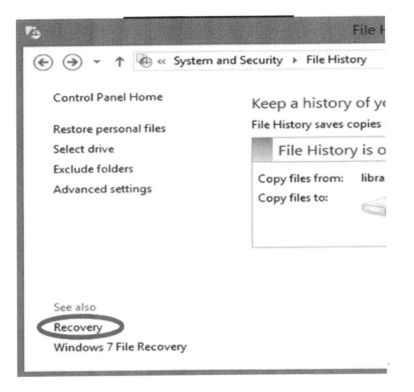

Click "Create a recovery drive." Then select "Create a system repair disc with CD or DVD."

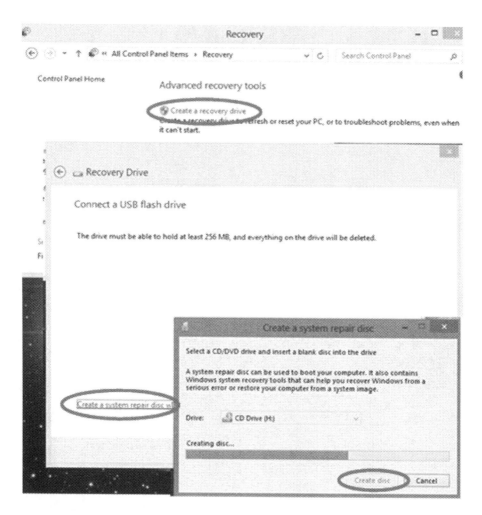

Insert a DVD into your DVD burner and click Create Disc. You can also use a USB stick if you prefer or if you don't have a DVD burner.

You will be able to start Windows with this disc if your computer fails.

Keep Your Computer Physically Clean

After constant use, your computer can get pretty dirty—dust on the monitor, grime and grease on the keyboard and mouse. It is good practice to keep all these components clean. We will take a look at some strategies and cleaning materials for cleaning different components.

Cleaning Keyboards

To clean your keyboard, unplug it from the computer, use a paper towel dabbed with rubbing alcohol (or diluted hand soap) and run the paper towel over the keys to remove all the dirt.

To clear dirt from in between the keys, a can of compressed air is a good method.

Cleaning Computer Mice

First, unplug your mouse from the computer. Older mice have a ball inside that tracks the movement; you can remove the ball by twisting the cover ring counter-clockwise.

Remove the ball and, with rubbing alcohol, rub it to remove dirt and grease. Also clean the little rollers inside with your paper towel.

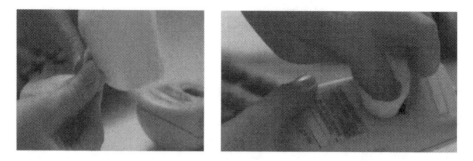

Put the cover back on and plug your mouse back in.

Newer mice are known as optical mice and do not have track balls. Cleaning these is much simpler. Unplug your mouse. Wipe the optical window with a paper towel and alcohol, as shown here.

Cleaning Your Monitor

Modern LCD screens can be quite fragile on the surface, so take care when cleaning the screen.

First, unplug the monitor from the main power and, with a soft cloth dampened with some diluted hand soap, start to gently wipe the surface, making sure you remove dust and finger marks.

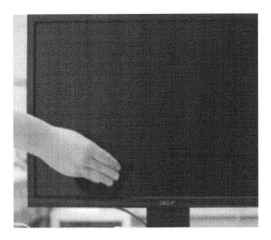

Dealing with Spills

If you spill liquid on a keyboard, the best thing I found to do is to quickly shut down the computer, disconnect the keyboard, and hold it upside down over a sink and allow the liquid to drain.

If the liquid is a fizzy drink, tea, or coffee, you will need to hold the keyboard on its side under warm running water to rinse off the sticky liquid.

At this point, the keyboard may not be repairable, but rinsing the sticky liquid off is the only chance for it to be usable again.

You will need to let the keyboard dry thoroughly for a few days before plugging it back in. After this kind of accident some keys may stick. This can be difficult to repair, depending on how bad the spill was. Fortunately, keyboards are cheap nowadays.

The best way to avoid this situation is to keep drinks away from the computer area.

Get the eBook for only $10!

Now you can take the weightless companion with you anywhere, anytime. Your purchase of this book entitles you to 3 electronic versions for only $10.

This Apress title will prove so indispensible that you'll want to carry it with you everywhere, which is why we are offering the eBook in 3 formats for only $10 if you have already purchased the print book.

Convenient and fully searchable, the PDF version enables you to easily find and copy code—or perform examples by quickly toggling between instructions and applications. The MOBI format is ideal for your Kindle, while the ePUB can be utilized on a variety of mobile devices.

Go to www.apress.com/promo/tendollars to purchase your companion eBook.

Apress®
THE EXPERT'S VOICE™